Teens Talk About
Anxiety and
Depression

Edited by Jennifer Landau

Featuring Q&As with Teen Health & Wellness's Dr. Jan

Rosen
YA

New York

Published in 2018 by The Rosen Publishing Group, Inc.
29 East 21st Street, New York, NY 10010

First Edition

Library of Congress Cataloging-in-Publication Data

Names: Landau, Jennifer, 1961– editor.
Title: Teens talk about anxiety and depression / edited by Jennifer Landau.
Description: New York : Rosen Publishing, 2018. | Series: Teen voices: real teens discuss real problems | Includes bibliographical references and index. | Audience: Grades 7–12.
Identifiers: LCCN 2017014691| ISBN 9781508176473 (library bound) | ISBN 9781508176558 (pbk.) | ISBN 9781508176312 (6 pack)
Subjects: LCSH: Anxiety in adolescence—Juvenile literature. | Depression in adolescence—Juvenile literature.
Classification: LCC RJ506.A58 L36 2018 | DDC 616.85/2700835—dc23
LC record available at https://lccn.loc.gov/2017014691

Manufactured in China

The content in this title has been compiled from The Rosen Publishing Group's Teen Health & Wellness digital platform. Additional original content was provided by Adam Furgang.

Contents

Introduction

Many teenagers suffer from anxiety and depression. However, they are often unable to understand their exact causes. Anxiety and depression are complex issues. Anxiety is generally defined as a feeling of worry or nervousness. In the field of psychiatry, anxiety is characterized as a nervous disorder that can result in panic attacks or self-destructive behaviors. Depression, in turn, is when a person is overcome with feelings of sadness. This sadness may be accompanied by a loss of interest in activities that he or she once found enjoyable. In clinical depression, these feelings of sadness last for a prolonged period of time.

Anxiety and depression can be caused by many factors. A person's confidence can fade when puberty hits and his or her body begins to change. This physical change can often be accompanied by uncomfortable and awkward feelings. Other issues with identity, especially sexual or gender identity, can also affect teens, making them feel confused or repressed, leading to anxiety or depression.

Depression and anxiety among teens has been increasing in recent years. These conditions are treatable, but only if teens get help.

Another major contributor to stress, anxiety, and depression is expectations from adults, including parents, teachers, and coaches. Teens also must deal with the expectations they set for themselves. When their expectations for high grades, popularity, confidence, or independence don't match their reality, teens may feel less in control of their lives and disappointed in themselves.

Anxiety can also stem from new and stressful experiences. Moving to a new part of the country, a new town, or even just starting in a new school can be enough to make anyone nervous. Other common stressors include fears of big crowds or participation in team sports. People who are introverted and prefer to do solo activities such as writing or making art might feel a crippling nervousness when having to pursue something that requires talking in public or interacting with crowds. The simple tasks of trying out to be a cheerleader or auditioning for a role in a school play may seem impossible to someone who suffers from anxiety.

Art can be a satisfying way to relieve anxiety and get your mind off of your problems. Some teens enjoy painting, while others may prefer photography or sculpture.

Even when friends and family support a teen's desire to try out for a sports team or go to a party, he or she may still feel unable to muster the courage needed to go after these goals.

Many teenagers experience anxiety or depression because of changes in their families, such as a divorce or separation between their parents or the loss of a loved one. According to the Childhood Domestic Violence Association, one in seven children will experience domestic violence at home. Children exposed to domestic violence are at greater risk for experiencing anxiety or becoming depressed.

One of the worst parts of anxiety and depression is that telling friends about these uncomfortable feelings might seem out of the question. When trying to talk to teachers or adults, the words might come out tangled or the subtleties of what is being expressed might get lost. It may feel like adults never seem to get it. If this is the case for you, know that you are not alone.

Share Your Own Story

The stories you are about to read were submitted by your peers to the Teen Health & Wellness Personal Story Project. Sharing stories is a powerful way to connect with other people. By sharing your story, you can connect with others who are dealing with these challenges. Find more information about how to submit your own story at the end of this resource.

While the specifics of any teen's situation are unique, the anxiety or depression one may be suffering as a result are not. According to the National Institute of Mental Health (NIMH), 12.5 percent of US teenagers between the ages of twelve and seventeen experienced at least one depressive episode in 2015. Furthermore, 25.1 percent of teenagers aged thirteen to eighteen experience anxiety.

While anxiety and depression are both entirely normal, if they start affecting a person's daily life and routines, they could be a more serious problem. Finding positive, rather than destructive, coping mechanisms can be very helpful. Opening up about your experiences with anxiety and depression can also be freeing. You will find that many others have shared similar experiences as you.

Chapter 1

Teens Talk About Anxiety

Many things can contribute to anxiety at home or at school. According to a 2017 article in the *Marysville Globe,* three students from Mountain View High School in Marysville, Washington, surveyed fellow students and found that as many as 88 percent of them were dealing with anxiety-related issues. Academics, especially

Academics can be a tremendous source of anxiety for a teen. Worrying about tests and homework assignments can make teens feel overwhelmed by stress.

homework-related pressures, factored heavily in their reports about anxiety.

Social media can also add to a teen's anxiety. FOMO, or fear of missing out, is an anxiety that someone has that something fun is happening somewhere else. It can be fueled by teens' addictive need to constantly check social media so they won't miss anything. The widespread use of mobile devices makes it easier to avoid face-to-face communication. According to a 2015 report by Common Sense Media, teens can spend as

It's important to take breaks from social media and mobile devices. Getting together with a friend is a positive way to unplug from the digital world.

many as nine hours a day with various forms of media or devices. When those face-to-face peer interactions do take place, they can be stressful because teens have less experience in social situations. But interacting with other people, no matter how uncomfortable you might feel, is important and allows for valuable social skills to develop.

Sometimes a solution for anxiety might include taking a short break from whatever it is that's making you anxious. If social media, a stressful household, or homework is causing anxiety, meeting up with a close friend in person could help. The library can be a great place to meet a friend or just sit alone and unwind. Once you get the break you need, you might find that you and your friends can help each other with whatever issues you're facing. Remember to seek guidance from peers, adults, and family. Once you find the courage to come forward, you will find help in managing your anxiety.

Presley's Story

Sweaty palms. Flushed skin. Quick breaths. You might think I'm describing a heart attack or stroke, but in reality, this is just my everyday experience ordering coffee. Or entering a large crowd. Or even talking aloud in front of an audience—that one is the worst. I've always been shy and bashful to a fault, and in recent years, I've started calling it what it is: anxiety. This isn't a story of miraculous recovery, but one of an ongoing process. Anxiety has ruled my life for a long time, but I refuse to let it hold me prisoner any longer.

For a long time, I lived in a box. I didn't make new friends, go to new places, or try new things. I was too afraid of others to really live my life. This all changed when I took Mrs. C.'s creative writing class my freshman year. We were encouraged to write a poem nearly every day and then to share it aloud. It took a lot of coaxing from Mrs. C., but one day, I did just that, and the response was unbelievable. People loved my poem!

Keeping a journal gives a teen a place to vent his or her feelings. Looking back on both positive and negative feelings can offer a way forward when dealing with tough issues.

They asked me questions about it and discussed it among themselves for a few minutes before she had to ask the class to quiet down. I was utterly bewildered—this went against everything I'd been internally telling myself. People didn't just irrationally hate me? I was capable of doing something meaningful and interesting? I soon took to writing like a college student takes to free dinner, and I found myself not only writing extra poems in Mrs. C.'s class, but also on my own in my spare time.

Predictably, my mom was ecstatic to find out I'd stepped outside of my comfort zone a bit and that I'd found a medium through which to express myself. But then, she asked me to do something unthinkable at the time—actually join the teen writer's group Mrs. C. had been mentioning to me enthusiastically over the past few weeks. If reading my poems aloud was stepping outside of my comfort zone, this was throwing it in the trash, going around the corner, and ordering a coffee. She and I bickered about the subject for months. Finally, sometime in late 2013, I was dropped off at our local library to attend my first meeting. Flash forward to today, and I'm begging my mom to let me walk there on the days she can't take me and I'm constantly trying to recruit new people to come.

Now, I'm not saying attending a writer's group has cured my anxiety. I still get an adrenaline rush just from answering questions aloud in class, and I still try to avoid large crowds whenever I can. However, having an intimate little group of people who I know genuinely like me and believe in me has made all the difference.

They've shown me that I don't need my peers' validation and that sometimes it's okay to stand alone. Through the writer's group and the support of my incredible friends and teachers, I'm learning to stand on my own two feet. And even though it's difficult, I do order a coffee on my own every Wednesday and Sunday. Maybe one day, I'll be confident enough to order one EVERY day of the week!

Ruby's Story

Academics are the way to success. If you understand your schoolwork and really put in the effort, you will succeed. My biggest challenge as a teen has been keeping up and focusing on academics. To me school doesn't come so easy. I have my weaknesses and strengths, but math has been my biggest struggle for sure. I know the embarrassment of sitting in class, getting called on, and feeling blank. They say getting called on is a learning experience, but it just scares me. It doesn't get worse than that.

Since I was young, numbers never went with me. I just could not understand them. The more I tried, the harder they got, and the more jumbled they became. I understand the panic and stress of getting a test back and seeing you failed. The previous week of studying day and night all gone to waste. The thing with math is if you don't understand one topic, you won't understand the rest because it is all linked together. When you are required to take three years of math in high school,

Being the focus of attention while giving a presentation in class can be an anxious experience for anyone. Practicing what you're going to say ahead of time will help you prepare and boost your confidence.

there's really not much you can do, other than trying your best and achieving the most that you can while you're at it. Math is a challenge that will be part of the rest of my life. School is great overall and I enjoy each and every class, other than math. Geometry, algebra, trigonometry, you name it. Without math, we would be nowhere in life and that's how I feel when I don't understand it.

MYTHS AND FACTS

MYTH Anxiety disorder is a single disorder that affects everyone the same way.

FACT There are many kinds of anxiety disorders, each with their own symptoms. These disorders include specific phobias, post-traumatic stress disorder, and obsessive-compulsive disorder.

MYTH People with no problems have no reason to feel depressed.

FACT Depression is an illness that is biologically based. Stresses that are not always obvious can cause depression. Support from friends and family can help with depression.

MYTH My anxiety disorder is part of my personality. I have to learn to live with it.

FACT Therapy and other supports can help you perceive things differently and teach you how to adopt a more positive attitude and change your behaviors.

Chapter 2

Teens Talk About Panic Attacks

Panic attacks can be very frightening. The Anxiety and Depression Association of America defines a panic attack as "the abrupt onset of intense fear or discomfort that reaches a peak within minutes." There can be many symptoms, including a racing heart, sweating, shaking, and shortness of breath, among others. Some panic attacks can even lead people to believe they might be having a heart attack.

Mild panic attacks can come and pass quickly. If panic attacks are

A panic attack can happen anywhere. Symptoms include a racing heart, sweating, shaking, and shortness of breath. Taking slow, deep breaths may lesson the severity of the attack.

happening frequently, you might be suffering from panic disorder. Seeking help from an adult and treatment from a professional may be necessary. The causes for panic attacks will vary from person to person, so treatment is often specialized. There are some steps a person can take to minimize the effects of a panic attack. Realizing that a panic attack is starting is the first step to lessening its effects. If you find yourself trembling, shaking, or short of breath, you could be having a panic attack. Slow breathing techniques can help calm you

Meditation and yoga are both helpful for relieving anxiety. Choose a favorite spot in your yard or at a local park to practice these relaxation techniques.

from what might feel like an intense situation. Repeating a favorite film or song quote during a panic attack or recalling a favorite moment in your life can help to distract from the stressful situation.

To help minimize future panic attacks, cut back on stressful situations, strive to eat a balanced, nutritious diet, avoid stimulants like sugar, coffee or other sources of caffeine, and practice relaxation techniques such as mediation or yoga. Exercising, getting enough sleep at night, and keeping socially active with supportive friends can also go a long way to help reduce or even avoid future panic attacks. Professional treatment for panic attacks can include therapy and sometimes medication.

Nathan's Story

It's April 17 and I wake up in a cold sweat. My room is dark and my eyes are having a hard time adjusting. I stumble to the restroom and wash my face. I decide my eyes are as ready as they will ever be, so I turn on the lights. It's blinding. My room is just how I left it when I went to sleep a few hours before. I walk out my door and poke my head in my parents' room. It appears to be empty. I stand at the top of the stairs. I flick the light switch and my eyes immediately jump to the dent in the wall at the bottom of the stairs where I've tripped and fallen so many times. I propel myself down the stairs, using the railings, skipping five or six steps as I fly down. I take a sharp right at the base of the stairs and enter the kitchen.

The kitchen lights are on so I can't see whether anyone is on the porch. Instinctively, I grab a pack of saltines (comfort food) from the pantry and walk toward the french doors. Before I can fully twist the handle, the door flies open and rain pours in. While struggling to slam the doors shut, lightning pierces through the limbs of the oak tree; ominous booms roll through. I frantically retrace my steps and begin to run to all of the closed doors in hopes of figuring out where my family is. After calling my dad, it get the voicemail message "Hi, I'm

Overreliance on mobile devices and social media can isolate teens and make face-to-face interactions more difficult. Teens should try to limit their time on these platforms.

unavailable right now, please call me back later." It's an echo of our relationship.

I try to think where they are—a concert, a movie, a play? It would explain why their phones are off. I'm mad. Why didn't they tell me they were leaving? Wait, I think to myself. Maybe they left me a note and I just missed it. I run upstairs and frantically search my parents' room. Nothing. While beginning to walk back downstairs, I hear a loud crash. I stop, frozen with fear. It sounded like a window had been broken. I drop to a crouched position on the stairs and slowly inch closer to the bottom steps. I am terrified of what might be around the corner. I peek my head around the wall to the left.

My brother's door is wide open and I can hear the storm pulsating as if it has life and rhythm. His room has many windows and is always illuminated. I take a deep breath and walk over to his door. His shelves are covered with trophies and sports gear. I see a tennis racket out of the corner of my eye. I grab it on my way through his doorway. I see the slivers of glass on the carpet. No evidence of what might have broken it. I hear another crash and feel shards of glass hit my skin. The cold wind sweeps into his room as I run for the stairs to my bedroom. I slam my door. All I can hear is loud thuds against the walls and the sound of windows occasionally smashing. I am hiding under the covers with a hole just big enough to see my doorway in case of intruders. It's hot under all my blankets, but I am too paralyzed with fear.

There are footsteps coming up the stairs. I do not know what to do except breathe harder and widen

The fear and discomfort associated with panic attacks can sometimes lead to arguments with parents or friends. During these fights, troublesome family issues may come to the surface.

my eyes. I grip the tennis racket until my hands hurt. Maybe they won't see me, maybe I'm hidden, maybe the lump of sheets will go unnoticed. I flood my brain with scenarios and outcomes of what might happen. These footsteps seem to take forever to reach my room. My doorknob starts twisting, things seem to slow down, and I feel the adrenaline as my heart races faster. I'm not quite able to make out what the intruder looks like, but he's large enough to be a man. He stands at my door and whispers my name. I gasp and throw the covers off of me in a heap of joy. My family is home.

They had been at a dinner party down the street. I yell and scream at my dad for not telling me. He tries to apologize and explain, but I don't let him. Telling him I hate him, I slam the door in his face.

Why am I mad at him? I felt relieved and overjoyed when they arrived and now I'm angry with him. I guess I was mad he forgot about me again.

Kayleigh's Story

I have anxiety and experience panic attacks. I also have to deal with depression, which comes from the anxiety, but that's a different story.

It all started on a horrible Sunday when both of my parents were working. We went to my grandma's house until my mom got out of work at 4 p.m. When my mom got to my grandma's house, she was light-headed and shaky because she hadn't eaten enough. She was having a mini panic attack for herself, too. I don't know what happened in my brain but suddenly I had a feeling of my throat closing. This feeling was not a surprise to me because I have many food allergies and I may have snuck a cookie or two. I spiraled into the worst panic attack in mankind (to me). I started breathing very heavily, my heart was racing, I was shaking uncontrollably, and I was extremely nauseous. I was shaking so badly that when I put my arm on the table, the glasses of water were shaking. With my mother and my grandmother worried about my health, we sped to the hospital.

After an hour of waiting, they told me I had a slight case of pneumonia just to get me out of there and threw an inhaler at me in case I had another attack. I followed up with my doctor, and he told me I was fine. He recommended a psychiatrist and was worried about my eating habits. Before all of the anxiety, I was a "chubby" 144 pounds. After a week or two of anxiety, I dropped to 116 pounds. If I had obtained this weight from healthy

Getting help from a trained professional such as a school counselor is an important step when dealing with anxiety and depression.

eating and exercise, it would be an accomplishment. I soon realized it happened because I was not eating. I have to force myself to eat at least two meals a day. Every single night, I have a panic attack that makes me want to run away and hide. When I feel the start of a panic attack, I try to fall asleep or just play with my fingers until I can't take it anymore and feel like I'm going insane. Only for the moment, though.

I have learned to open up with my mom, and she promises to get me help so I am ready for our trip to Florida and then Canada. I understand I can't live off of Campbell's chicken noodle soup for weeks on end. My advice to all of the depressed and anxious and teens with eating disorders is that no matter how hard it gets, you have to keep pushing through. Another thing is that if you experience anything this bad, you should tell somebody and get help. Don't wait until it is too late.

I hope you have learned something from my story. I wish you luck and my support goes to you. Rise against!

Ask Dr. Jan

Dear Dr. Jan,
Recently I told my dad that I was feeling stressed out. He said that I'm too young at seventeen to be stressed. Is that true?

—Yipeng

Dear Yipeng,

Unfortunately, adults often underestimate the amount of stress that young people experience. High school is a particularly stressful time in terms of social, emotional, and academic pressures. Often parents assume that because you're young, not working a full-time job, and/or raising a family, that you have nothing to be stressed about. As you know, this is simply not true. The teen years are actually one of the most stressful stages of a person's lifetime.

The good news is that there are many ways to manage stress. One option is to evaluate your daily activities. Are you overbooked with too many after-school activities? If you have some free time after school, consider taking a yoga class or learning how to meditate. Research shows that meditation can significantly reduce stress. There are also a variety of easy-to-learn relaxation techniques. These include deep breathing (breathing in deeply, holding your breath for a second or two, and breathing out slowly) and visual imagery (closing your eyes and imagining yourself in a relaxing place, focusing your mind on all the details of this place). In addition, physical exercise has been found to be beneficial.

If you feel like relaxation techniques aren't enough, consider visiting a therapist. In addition to teaching relaxation techniques, mental health professionals can also help with a variety of other strategies, including changing thinking patterns, which often fuel feelings of stress. While no one can live stress free, there's a lot that you can do to better manage your stress.

Chapter 3

Teens Talk About Self-Harm and Depression

Most everyone feels sad or unhappy at some point. However, if you are often feeling sad with no clear cause, you might be depressed. According to the Anxiety and Depression Association of America, it is not uncommon for people with depression to have suffered from anxiety at some point in their past. Although one disorder does not lead to the other, many people suffer from both anxiety and depression.

Self-harm is the practice of injuring yourself in order to relieve emotional pain or distress. Cutting and burning oneself are the most common forms of self-harm. There are many causes of self-harm, including stress from school, problems at home, peer pressure, and too much time in front of media or a computer, where teens are fed idealized depictions of how to look and behave.

Self-harming is often concealed and done in private, so it's important to realize that the behavior is only masking another problem. It might seem hard to do, but the first step to recovery from depression or self-harm is telling a friend, parent, or another adult what you are

If a teen keeps his or her depression or self-harm a secret, it is difficult to deal with the underlying issues. Confiding in a loved one can help ease the burden.

going through. Treatment for depression and self-harm from a professional therapist will be necessary.

Severe depression that is untreated can lead to suicidal thoughts. Suicide among teenagers is a serious problem. According to a 2015 fact sheet by the Centers for Disease Control and Prevention (CDC), in 2013 suicide was the second-leading cause of death among persons aged fifteen to twenty-four. Seeking help from a doctor or therapist trained to work with those suffering from depression is important. With therapy, and sometimes medication, depression can be brought under control.

Note: This section will discuss details of a sexual assault. If such content may make you uncomfortable, please continue on to the following section.

Jazmyn's Story

Growing up, life wasn't always easy. My family and I lived in poverty. An alcoholic and abusive father didn't make it any easier. Even at a young age I was aware of that. Even after my mother got up enough strength to leave him and never look back, we struggled. Things started to look up when we moved to Wisconsin to be closer to my grandparents when I was eight, but it was short lived. It was there that I was exposed to public school and introduced to popularity and peer pressure. It was hard, but I managed to make my way through elementary and middle school with little to no problems.

But high school was different. I had suddenly become a target for bullies, and I couldn't figure out why. I wasn't different from the other kids and tried my hardest to lay low and be like everyone else. That didn't stop kids from teasing me, hitting me, and pushing me in the hallways. All of this on top of the stress of my first year of high school began to wear away at me. I slowly fell into a pit of depression. I went from crying myself to sleep every night, to wishing that I could cry, but all I could do was feel numb. I began cutting to try to relieve some emotional pain or to simply feel something, with little to no luck.

Bullying is a serious problem because it can isolate a teen, causing stress that can lead to bouts of depression.

My tipping point was one day in math class. Out of nowhere, one of the guys spoke up. "Jazmyn, why are you still here?" he said, followed by some chuckles from the group of guys he was sitting with. "Why haven't you committed suicide yet? We all know you would look better hanging from a tree" (which is a reference to when they used to hang or lynch slaves because I'm African American). After that, I couldn't take it anymore. I started thinking that I really was better off dead.

I went home that day and attempted suicide for the first time. I looked on the back of the pill bottle to make sure I knew the safe amount of pills to take, and I doubled it. Then I quietly lied down on my bed and fell asleep expecting to not wake up, but I did. That one attempt would soon turn into twelve. Each time, I multiplied the number of pills I consumed. I could have easily died at attempt number two, but something kept me alive.

Eventually, a teacher saw my cut marks and was obligated to report it. My family was called in, and they brought me to rehab to get help. After seven days of learning to cope and deal with my feelings, life truly started to look up. That is until I went to school the next day. I was sexually assaulted by a student at my school. I'll spare you the details, but it was traumatizing nonetheless. When I finally got up the courage to report it the next day, the school officials did not handle it professionally at all. They

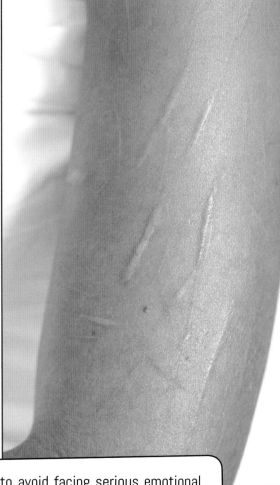

Many teens self-harm as a way to avoid facing serious emotional problems. In order to recover, a teen must deal with the issues that are leading to this dangerous behavior.

suspended us both because he claimed that I "wanted it." That was when my life changed.

My mom took my siblings and I out of school and we went to school board meetings, boycotted the school, and tried to share what had happened with as many people as we could so they would be aware of what kind of school their children were attending. Other stories surfaced of students being mistreated, and the school failing to report things to authorities that should have been reported, but nothing we did could take back what I had gone through. Most of the school sided with my assaulter. Why wouldn't they? He was the popular jock and the head of every sports team. The school NEEDED him for grants, so he got to keep his life while mine was turned upside down. On top of all that, HE got a restraining order against ME.

I remembered what I had learned in rehab, though, and didn't relapse into self-harm, but I decided to go to a party with a girl who I THOUGHT was my friend to take my mind off of things. At the party, someone spiked the beverage I was drinking and I ended up blacking out and getting taken advantage of. The girl I had gone to the party with? Her mom found out about the party and called the police. They cut a deal with her that she wouldn't get in trouble if she narced on everyone there, and she took it in a heartbeat. In her version of the story, I willingly slept with the guy who had taken advantage of me. The police wanted to charge me with sexual assault of a child because we were both under the age of eighteen.

The next few months were filled with court appearances and restraining order hearings. People continually made me recount the horrible, traumatizing memories to try to slip me up. Eventually, I got a deal that if I completed six months of probation they would clean my record. I completed that with no problems and thought things were finally going my way. That is, until my boyfriend dumped me on my sixteenth birthday (ouch!). After that, I fell into a three-month depression.

One day, I just looked in the mirror and said "You know what? Everyone who's ever done me wrong? It's their loss! No one is going to respect me if I don't respect myself!" I started doing research online on how to live a healthier life. I began eating healthier and working out. Immediately, I started to feel more confident and proud of myself. I began training for my first 5k race.

Over the next few months, I fell in love with running and exercising. It made me feel amazing, and knowing I was taking

Getting involved in a sport or exercise routine can relieve stress and boost self-esteem as long as it is done in moderation.

care of myself was a bonus! A few months later, I went to a camp and ended up getting saved and going to church. I went from being a lonely, insecure little girl to a strong and inspirational woman. I made a vow to use my story to help other people and started a support group in my community where I teach kids and teens about key experiences teens go through and how to deal with them. I also started my own personal growth campaign that enables kids and teens to stand up to the stigmas society puts on them and decide whom they want to be. Starting in September, I will be traveling from school to school doing presentations. Also this September I will be competing for Miss Wisconsin Teen USA, and if I win I will be moving on to the Miss Teen USA competition in the Bahamas. I wouldn't be who I am today without my struggles.

Yamilet's Story

I've had to overcome many things throughout my life, but the biggest obstacle was overcoming depression. Being in a depression has been one of my biggest fears because when my dark thoughts took over, I didn't know what to expect. It changed my life completely. I self-harmed multiple times, I was hospitalized, and had negative thoughts.

Self-harming wasn't something I joked about. It was my way out of stress and sadness. My parents' separation affected me badly, and it gave me more reasons to harm myself. Cutting myself changed me because I got addicted to doing it and it left permanent marks. I went from cutting once in a while to cutting day after day. The cuts got deeper and deeper each time, and I was afraid that one of those cuts would end everything. Being in a depression scared me so much because it gave me reasons to harm myself.

Hurting myself led to me being hospitalized twice. I thought I learned my lesson when I took an overdose of pills. I was in the hospital for three days, and every day that passed I felt my body giving up. When this happened, my mom and dad soon realized that I was depressed. The doctors prescribed some antidepressants and they worked for a while. Seven months passed, and I still continued to harm myself and my depression was getting worse every day. Being hospitalized didn't work. The self-harm continued and my negative thoughts took over many times. I was later put in the Palmetto Baptist Mental Hospital in Columbia. The therapies and strategies seemed to help. My thoughts were my biggest problem. No matter what I did, they would overpower me. I felt worthless and no good for this world. The more I tried forgetting about the thoughts, the more they came back. It got to the point where I got tired of them all.

This depression taught me a lot about life and myself. What I learned was that no matter what comes in life, I'm the one who makes it the way it is. I realized that I'm way stronger than I thought I was. Harming myself was never the answer because it could've ended everything. The advice I'd give to someone with depression is to never give up, to never lose hope, and to always stay strong. I was depressed for three years and still am, but keeping my head up has helped me a lot. Going to weekly therapy and using a variety of skills has helped me stay harm free and beat depression. If I can do this, anyone else can, as long as they believe in themselves.

Lindsay's Story

Everyone remembers their first time. The suspense of sitting there, making this decision. How would it feel? Will it make me feel better? Will I regret this? Horrible. No. Yes. The deciding factor that pushes you over the edge is so vividly etched into your mind, just like the marks on your skin. Self-harm has made thousands of people feel like worn-out and beaten-up books. Books that have faded into the back of the shelves lining the story-filled rooms, being overshadowed by the *New York Times* best sellers. I saw myself as one of those books. A book that made a great paperweight or coaster for someone's morning coffee, but not worth the read.

Psychologist Erik Erikson believed that people had eight different developmental stages that occurred throughout the human lifespan. From five to twelve is considered the industry versus inferiority stage. This is illustrated by emphasizing the significance of the peer group of a child. Industry in a child's development shows that praise and encouragement help children achieve their goals. On the other end, feelings of inferiority are constructed by failure in social situations, and lack of encouragement. This is a crucial stage for adolescents. That feeling of inferiority extends beyond the age range. Growing up, I was always seen

When teens feel left out of a group of friends, that sense of rejection can lead to depression and low self-esteem.

as second best. The silver medal, the almost but not quite. Being compared to a better version of me with shuffled-up DNA. Inferiority reached out to not only my home situation, but also my social life. The pushover. The add-on. I was always the one who was included when it was for their benefit. The inferiority grew as time progressed. I was the secondhand book that was bought to fill the shelves.

I saw my existence as being alive, but not feeling a living sense in my body. Each day was routine and chipped away at my self-worth. Nothing had ever really made me feel wanted or feel more than what I had made myself out to be. Hearing about self-harm for the first time was alarming. Having a low pain tolerance, it did not make sense that depressed teenagers would toy with this receptor deliberately. The thought of self-harm was planted in my head shortly thereafter, and I wondered what repetitively hurting themselves did for these teenagers. It was not until I found a friend to enlighten me that I understood why someone who was depressed would gash her skin in order to cope. She told me how it made her feel. That it released stress and made her feel less sad. She illustrated self-harm as if it was a solution to my problems. I had never considered it until one day after school when I was feeling more empty than usual. I sat there with a blade, debating how this would change my life. I told myself I was better than this, that I had more ways than this to help me, but it wasn't enough. I continued to self-harm for three years, covering my body with slashes and wearing long sleeves to conceal the battle wounds.

I don't know exactly what the turning point was for me to stop doing this. I had quite possibly driven myself to the last dead end of the accessible roads just to realize that driving through a route with no outlet was not beneficial for my progression in the journey. It took me a long time to realize that self-harm had made me feel worse than when I started. I decided it was time to stop and try to be happy. I threw away anything I could use to initiate the itching feeling of self-harm and told myself that I had spent so long being miserable that it was starting to consume me. Every day, I worked on being happy again. I gave myself compliments, even if I didn't believe them fully at the time. I started doing things to make me happy. Within weeks of practicing healthy habits, I felt a surge of energy in myself. And ever since I decided that being happy was worth more, I have been happier.

I know that I cannot preach this to everyone because not everyone will listen. People who are cursed with depression constantly hear the perpetual speeches of how it gets better. It is not rational to ask someone to listen to the same speech that person has heard thousands of times. The tunnel vision has a light at the end for a reason. You are not your mental illness or your mistakes. I can't convince anyone who is depressed that life really is not what you think it is. But I am here to say I am glad that I overcame my illness. I realized that even though I might be a book that is not read, it does not make the message inside me any less important. There are people out there who find my story amazing and heartwarming. The book that I am is enjoyed by someone out there, and that is enough for me to keep my story alive.

People may not see themselves as important or beneficial to society, but being out of sight can mean being out of mind. Not all people with depression can pick themselves up every day and tell themselves that their book is worth the read. But there is always that one day. That one day when the light at the end of the tunnel is closer, warmer, and liberating. The end of the tunnel is not the end of your story, but the end to feelings of darkness. The way to feel alive is to establish a routine that makes you feel like living. Just think about that one day and how you will feel when the sadness clears up and the light comes on.

Steff's Story

When I was younger, I once described depression as looking up at the night sky. On that night, there would be no stars, and there would be no moon. There would be no light at all. Just... darkness. For the longest time, it seemed as if my life was inhabited by that darkness. I found myself spiraling down emotionally and mentally. I may have retained my grades, but I feared that I was ultimately losing myself... After all, what was my purpose? What was the purpose of life?

I discovered my purpose when I finally opened an email from my best friend. I had known her for years, and I believed that I knew her better than the back of my hand. And yet, I never knew—until then—that she had been raped. That for all these years, she's been cutting herself, burning herself, injuring herself to deal with that horrid hidden truth. This was the first time that she had told someone, and she begged me to keep it quiet. "It's my secret, " she told me. "It's my past. My darkness."

This newly shared secret should have shattered me— the final straw. It should have sent me spiraling back down into that eternal abyss. But instead, she inspired me to speak up for all of us—for all those who self-harm.

My involvement with this controversial, taboo subject began last year with a discussion between my old therapist and me. My passion to help others soon translated into an internship with the new psychotherapeutic organization Balance Healing Group, LLC. As their very first intern, I am currently tasked with the responsibilities of research, website maintenance, and my own personal project: the creation and development of a peer mentoring program for suicidal and depressed teenagers.

With the encouragement and support of the organizational staff, I have brought this contemporary, controversial issue to the forefront of academic institutions by meeting with my principal and guidance counselor. I explained to them the issue of self-harm—its prevalence and growing popularity among our students—and how I could help. Since that meeting, I have been in the process of formulating and conducting a project, a presentation that speaks of the darkness within each and every one of us. So far, I have spoken in front of small groups of peers, helping them to understand self-harm: what it is, why we do it, and how we can learn to help ourselves.

In March, which is Self-Injury Awareness Month, I will give a presentation to the students and staff of my high school and middle school. My goal is to promote a build-off initiative of Project Purple, an official nationwide project established by former NBA star Chris Herren. Like Herren, my message is already beginning to spread. In the coming spring, I will be presenting at other local high schools and middle schools. Their hope—and my goal—is to establish a new mind-set regarding self-harm by offering myself as an example. With each and every presentation, I speak from my heart, telling my own story of the darkness: how I had fallen into depression, how I

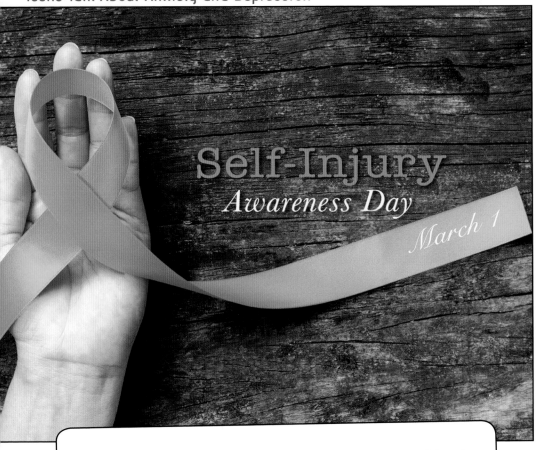

Self-Injury
Awareness Day
March 1

March 1 is National Self-Injury Awareness Day. An orange ribbon is worn as a symbol of hope and support for those who self-harm.

relied on the infamous "coping" methods, and how I looked up at the night sky and, finally, saw the stars at last.

As an ex-cutter, I knew that my words would mean so much more to the student body. I am not another forty-year-old lecturing on the effects it will have on our chances in the job market. I am one of them—one of the students. I, too, face the daily pressures of school and home and, at first, I resorted to those coping methods. Now, however, I have learned to not only overcome them, but also to utilize the darkness of my

Who to Call

The following hotlines offer support for those dealing with anxiety and depression:

Depression and Bipolar Support
800-273-TALK
http://www.dbsalliance.org
Twenty-four hours a day, seven days a week

National Hopeline Network
800-442-HOPE
http://www.hopeline.com
Twenty-four hours a day, seven days a week

Suicide Hotlines Listing by State
http://www.suicidehotlines.com

National Institute of Mental Health Information Center
866-615-6464
http://www.nimh.nih.gov
8 a.m. to 8 p.m. EST, Monday to Friday

National Mental Health Association Hotline
800-273-TALK
http://www.nhma.org
Twenty-four hours a day, seven days a week

past to promote light in the future. My purpose is to demonstrate that you are not alone, that self-harm is not your only option, and that there is always light in this "world of darkness. "

Chapter 4

Teens Talk About Helping a Depressed Friend

Everyone needs help from a friend sometimes. Knowing the signs of depression can help you recognize when a friend needs your support. People who are depressed might suddenly feel sad or angry. A friend who is depressed may also change his behavior and withdraw from his usual activities. Other symptoms of depression may be poor grades, a change in eating habits, drug or alcohol use, and bouts of crying. Depressed people will sometimes talk about suicide.

If you suspect a friend is depressed, the first step to take is to talk to that person and let her know you are there for her. Helping a friend who is depressed requires patience and understanding. Do not be tough on the person or talk down to her. Remember that she needs help, not judgment. Having a caring and sympathetic attitude may help your friend open up and talk. Remember that being a good friend means being there when life gets tough, not just during the good times.

If you suspect your friend is engaging in dangerous behavior or is possibly suicidal, you should tell an adult or teacher right away. In school, a teacher, guidance

Talking with a teacher or counselor may help a teen suffering from depression or anxiety find a new way of looking at the root causes of his or her mental health concerns.

counselor, or teacher's aide can help. At home, tell your parents or your friend's parents. Even if you might be breaking your friend's confidence, it's important to act if you suspect he might be in danger. Crisis Text Line offers a free help line to those in need of immediate support. Anyone can text "Connect" to 741741 and speak to trained crisis counselors about any topic.

Kylie's Story

When I was in the sixth grade, I was misinformed about depression. I believed that people with depression had weak minds and weren't strong. I also believed that talking to someone about one's problems, or even listening to the words a depressed person had to say, would be utterly pointless. People who were suicidal were ungrateful and throwing their lives away. I now acknowledge that was an unseemly and ignorant way to think.

The first time I encountered depression was in the seventh grade. My close friend and I had just finished playing a modified version of tag. It was a very hot day, but we were both energetic. We had decided to cool down during what was left of our thirty-minute recess. Right after we sat on the concrete ground, we were already laughing hysterically. I did not know that as we laughed, and as she smiled, she was hiding her sadness and fear.

Yet, for a split second, I glanced at her wrist and saw the thing, inch-long scars on her arm. "What happened?" I asked and grabbed her by the wrist. The smile that seemed to always be on her face faded and she looked oddly dejected. We were very close, and I am sure she anticipated me finding out eventually. But I wasn't sure if she wanted me to find out then and there.

"I'll tell you later," she whispered. But I knew we had no more classes together, and because of our strict parents we both had to go straight home. Nevertheless, I decided not to rush her or force her to tell me. I hoped she'd tell me if she ever felt comfortable.

The next day, I tried my best to ignore what I had seen. I didn't bring it up. When recess came, we purposely walked after the horde of excited children.

And when we were almost outside, we intentionally took a detour and walked to the restroom, even though we didn't have to actually use it. I remember, she sat in the windowsill and gave me a weak smile.

"It helps," was what she first told me.

"Doesn't it hurt?"

"No. It just helps."

Honestly, I couldn't understand what she meant. How could cutting through your skin help with anything? Even now, I'm not entirely sure. But I think the pain she

If your friend is self-harming, offer support without judgment. Thank your friend for confiding in you and make it clear you are willing to be there as he or she heads down the path toward healing.

inflicted on her arm helped her forget her other pains. Maybe it's something deeper than that. She explained the problems she had and the abuse she had been tolerating. I simply listened and occasionally nodded so she would know I was still listening. For thirty minutes, we sat in the reeking bathroom, but I didn't really mind because that's what friends do.

One day, I told her to go to the guidance counselor. I figured the guidance counselor could help more than a child such as myself. Simply put, we were kids. There's only so much children can do before needing an adult's help.

"I don't trust them, they'll tell my mom everything I said."

All I did was nod.

I know that I didn't help her as well as I could. I listened when she had something to say and comforted her when she cried. However, not once was I able to successfully get adult help. I felt that it would betray her trust, and I honestly didn't want to be hated by my best friend. I think that makes me an ignorant person. I was too self-absorbed and too worried about ruining our friendship to realize that her life was at stake.

I wasn't the best help around. But I feel that the little things I did, like listening, and simply being there, mattered. I wish I could have gotten her the help she needed when I interacted with her, but I suppose it's too late now. After we graduated from middle school and after we had gotten to the point where we felt like sisters, she was forbidden to contact anyone. Everything we could have used to still keep in touch was taken away or controlled to the point where if I sent one email, I'm sure she would get in trouble with her mother. Sadly, I don't know if she still cries herself to sleep.

But now I know that depressed people don't purposely feel the way they do. I understand why someone might want to commit suicide, although I won't encourage it. And I won't judge someone by saying that person isn't "strong" because we're all exposed to different situations and we all interpret things differently. In conclusion, there's a good chance that I won't ever see that friend again. But if I ever do, I wouldn't mind sitting down and listening to what she has to say.

10 Great Questions
to Ask a Psychiatrist

1. I've tried talking to my friends and family about my problems but still feel frustrated and helpless. What should I do now?

2. I think my friend might be suicidal. What if I get help but I was wrong and she is angry with me?

3. My anxiety is keeping me from doing the things I want to do. How can I change my behavior?

4. I feel sad most of the time, but I'm not sure why. What can I do to feel better?

5. I don't enjoy doing much of anything anymore. Have my tastes changed or could I be depressed?

6. I have been self-harming myself. What steps should I take to stop?

7. Is depression a disease that someone can recover from, like the flu?

8. If I am depressed, should I be worried that I will become suicidal?

9. My house is a very stressful environment that I am unable to avoid. What can I do to help my situation?

10. What is the difference between a panic attack and an anxiety disorder?

The Teen Health & Wellness Personal Story Project

Be part of the Teen Health & Wellness Personal Story Project and share your story about successfully dealing with or overcoming a challenge. If your story is accepted for online publication, it will be posted on the Teen Health & Wellness site and featured on its homepage. You will also receive a certificate of achievement from Rosen Publishing and a $25 gift certificate to Barnes & Noble or Chapters.

Sharing stories is a powerful way to connect with other people. By sharing your story, you can connect with others who are dealing with these challenges. Visit teenhealthandwellness.com/static/personalstoryproject to read other teens' stories and to submit your own.

Scan this QR code to go to the Personal Story Project homepage.

Glossary

addictive Causing a physical or emotional dependency.

antidepressant A drug meant to alleviate the symptoms of depression.

depression A condition characterized by feelings of sadness, inadequacy, or low spirits.

mentor An experienced and trusted person who can help and advise a less experienced learner.

obsessive-compulsive disorder A disorder that causes uncontrollable thoughts and behaviors.

panic attack A sudden feeling of intense anxiety with symptoms such as sweating and shortness of breath.

phobia An extreme fear or an irrational need to avoid something.

post-traumatic stress disorder A condition characterized by mental or emotional stress that follows a shocking or disturbing life event.

psychiatrist A medical doctor specializing in the treatment of mental illness.

psychotherapeutic Treating a mental disorder through talking about problems that are causing distress.

self-harm Deliberate injury to oneself to relieve emotional pain or stress.

stressful Causing intense emotional or mental pressure.

suicide The act of intentionally killing oneself.

textline A hotline for people in need, accessed through texting instead of calling on a phone.

therapy A treatment designed to heal a particular disorder.

For More Information

American Academy of Child & Adolescent Psychiatry (AACAP)
3615 Wisconsin Avenue NW
Washington, DC 20016
(202) 966-7300
Website: https://www.aacap.org
Facebook: @American-Academy-of-Child-Adolescent-Psychiatry
Twitter: @aacap
The AACAP encourages healthy child, adolescent, and family development through the use of education, research, and advocacy programs.

American Foundation for Suicide Prevention (AFSP)
120 Wall Street, 29th floor
New York, NY 10005
(888) 333-2377
Website: https://www.afsp.org
Facebook: @afspnational
Twitter: @afspnational
Instagram: @afspnational
The AFSP funds scientific research about suicide and suicide prevention, as well as providing resources and aid to those affected by suicide.

Canadian Mental Health Association (CMHA)
500-250 Dundas Street
West Toronto, ON M5T 2Z5
Canada
(613) 745-7750
Website: http://www.cmha.ca
Facebook: @CMHANational
Twitter: @CMHA_NTL
CMHA is a national charity organization that improves
    mental health for Canadians through community-
    based support resources.

Center for Addiction and Mental Health (CAMH)
    Foundation
Bell Gateway Building
100 Stokes Street, 5th floor
Toronto, ON M6J 1H4
Canada
(416) 979-6909
Website: https://www.supportcamh.ca
Facebook: @end.stigma
Twitter: @endstigma
Instagram: @camhfoundation
CAMH is one of the largest hospitals in North America
    that specializes in mental illness and health for both
    inpatient and outpatient care.

National Alliance on Mental Illness (NAMI)
3803 N. Fairfax Drive, Suite 100
Arlington, VA 22203
(703) 524-7600

Website: https://www.nami.org
Facebook: @NAMI
Twitter: @namicommunicate
Instagram: @NAMICommunicate
NAMI is an organization dedicated to education,
    advocacy programs, and public policy regarding
    mental health.

National Institute of Mental Health (NIMH)
6001 Executive Boulevard, Room 6200 MSC 9663
Bethesda, MD 20892
(866) 615-6464
Website: https://www.nimh.nih.gov
Facebook: @nimhgov
Twitter: @nimhgov
NIMH is a federal agency dedicated to research about
    mental health disorders. It is part of the US
    Department of Health and Human Services.

Teen Health & Wellness
29 East 21st Street
New York, NY 10010
(877) 381-6649
Website: http://www.teenhealthandwellness.com
App: Teen Hotlines
Teen Health & Wellness provides nonjudgmental,
    straightforward, curricular and self-help support
    on topics such as diseases, drugs and alcohol,
    nutrition, mental health, suicide and bullying,
    green living, and LGBTQ+ issues. Its free Teen
    Hotlines app provides a concise list of hotlines,

help lines, and information lines on the subjects
that affect teens most.

Websites

Because of the changing nature of internet links,
Rosen Publishing has developed an online list of
websites related to the subject of this book. This site
is updated regularly. Please use this link to access
this list:

http://www.rosenlinks.com/TNV/Anxiety

For Further Reading

Bradshaw, Cheryl M. *How to Like Yourself: A Teen's Guide to Quieting Your Inner Critic and Building Lasting Self-Esteem.* Oakland, CA: Instant Help, 2016.

Kurtz, Adam J. *Pick Me Up: A Pep Talk for Now and Later.* New York, NY: TarcherPerigee, 2016.

Lin, Y. S. *Defeating Depression.* (Effective Survival Strategies). New York, NY: Rosen Publishing, 2016.

McDonagh, Thomas, and Jon Patrick Hatcher. *101 Ways to Conquer Teen Anxiety: Simple Tips, Techniques and Strategies for Overcoming Anxiety, Worry and Panic Attacks.* Berkeley, CA: Ulysses Press, 2016.

Porterfield, Jason. *Teen Stress and Anxiety.* (Teen Mental Health). New York, NY: Rosen Publishing, 2014.

Roberts, Emily. *Express Yourself: A Teen Girl's Guide to Speaking Up and Being Who You Are.* Oakland, CA: Instant Help, 2015.

Schab, Lisa M. *Self-Esteem for Teens: Six Principles for Creating the Life You Want.* Oakland, CA: Instant Help, 2015.

Shannon, Jennifer. *The Anxiety Survival Guide for Teens: CBT Skills to Overcome Fear, Worry, and Panic.* Oakland, CA: Instant Help, 2015.

Staley, Erin. *Defeating Stress and Anxiety.* (Effective Survival Strategies). New York, NY: Rosen Publishing, 2016.

Vo, Dzung X. *The Mindful Teen: Powerful Skills to Help You Handle Stress One Moment at a Time.* Oakland, CA: Instant Help, 2015.

Wells, Polly, and Peter Mitchell. *Freaking Out: Real-life Stories About Anxiety.* Toronto, Ontario: Annick Press, 2013.

Willard, Christopher. *Mindfulness for Teen Anxiety: A Workbook for Overcoming Anxiety at Home, at School, and Everywhere Else.* Oakland, CA: Instant Help, 2014.

Bibliography

Anxiety and Depression Association of America. "Understanding the Facts: Depression." Retrieved February 17, 2017. https://www.adaa.org /understanding-anxiety/depression.

Centers for Disease Control and Prevention. "Suicide Prevention." October 28, 2016. https://www.cdc.gov/ ViolencePrevention/suicide/index.html.

Common Sense Media. "The Common Sense Census: Media Use by Tweens and Teens." Retrieved February 15, 2017.http://static1.1.sqspcdn.com /static/f/1083077/26645197/1446492628567 /CSM_TeenTween_MediaCensus_FinalWebVersion_1 .pdf.

Crisis Text Line. "Text 'Connect' to 741741." Retrieved February 15, 2017. http://www.crisistextline.org.

Elements Behavioral Health. "Teens Are Feeling More Anxious Than Ever." Retrieved February 28, 2017. https://www.elementsbehavioralhealth.com/featured /teenagers-are-feeling-more-anxious-than-ever.

"Jazmyn's Story." April 2017. http://www. teenhealthandwellness.com/article/119/11 /jazmyns-story.

"Kayleigh's Story." Teen Health and Wellness. October 2016. http://www.teenhealthandwellness.com /article/47/9/kayleighs-story.

"Kylie's Story." Teen Health and Wellness. April 2017. http://www.teenhealthandwellness.com/article/119 /12/kylies-story.

"Lindsay's Story." "Teen Health and Wellness."
September 2016. http://www.teenhealthandwellness
.com/article/294/10/lindsays-story

"Nathan's Story." Teen Health and Wellness. October
2016. http://www.teenhealthandwellness.com
/article/47/7/nathans-story.

National Institute of Mental Health. "Any Anxiety Disorder
Among Adults." Retrieved February 17, 2017.
https://www.nimh.nih.gov/health/statistics/
prevalence/any-anxiety-disorder-among-adults.shtml.

"Presley's Story." Teen Health and Wellness. October
2016. http://www.teenhealthandwellness.com
/article/47/11/presleys-story

Powell, Steve. "Teens Know All Too Much About
Anxiety." *Marysville Globe.* February 16, 2017. http://
www.marysvilleglobe.com/life
/teens-know-all-too-much-about-anxiety.

Puckett, Lily. "Do THIS the Next Time You Have a Panic
Attack." TeenVogue.com. May 29, 2016.
http://www.teenvogue.com/story/
panic-attacks-how-to-calm-down.

"Ruby's Story." Teen Health and Wellness. November
2015. http://www.teenhealthandwellness.com
/article/28/8/rubys-story.

"Steff's Story." Teen Health and Wellness. September
2016. http://www.teenhealthandwellness.com
/article/294/11/steffs-story.

"Yamilet's Story." Teen Health and Wellness. September
2016. http://www.teenhealthandwellness.com/
article/294/12/yamilets-story.

Index

high school, 14, 29, 41

I

introvert, 6

J

Jazmyn, 29–34

K

Kayleigh, 23–25
Kylie, 45–49

L

Lindsay, 36–40

M

March, 41
Marysville Globe, 9
medication, 19, 29
meditation, 19, 26
mental illness, 39
mentor, 41
Miss Teen USA, 34
Miss Wisconsin Teen USA, 34
Mountain View High School, 9

N

Nathan, 20–23

National Institute of Mental Health, (NIMH), 8

O

obsessive-compulsive disorder, 16

P

Palmetto Baptist Mental Hospital, 35
panic attacks, 4, 17–25
peer, 7, 11, 14, 27, 29, 36, 41
personality, 16
phobia, 16
poems, 12–13
post-traumatic stress disorder, 16
Presley, 11–14
Project Purple, 41
psychiatrist, 25
psychotherapy, 41
puberty, 4

R

racing heart, 17, 22
relaxation techniques, 19, 26
Ruby, 14–15

S

self-harm, 27–43

About the Editor

Jennifer Landau is an author and editor who has written about psychological bullying, cybercitizenship, and drug and alcohol abuse, among other topics. She has an MA in English from New York University and an MST in general and special education from Fordham University. Landau has taught writing to young children, teens, and seniors.

About Dr. Jan

Dr. Jan Hittelman, a licensed psychologist with over thirty years experience working with children and families, has authored monthly columns for the *Daily Camera*, Boulder Valley School District, and online for the Rosen Publishing Group. He is the founder of the Boulder Counseling Cooperative and the director of Boulder Psychological Services.

Photo Credits

Cover Sabphoto/Shutterstock.com; p. 5 Diego Cervo/Shutterstock.com; p. 6 © iStockphoto.com/kamil; p. 9 Kristy-Anne Glubish/Getty Images; p. 10 Martin Dimitrov/E+/Getty Images; p. 12 pickingpok/Shutterstock.com; p. 15 PhotoAlto/Sigrid Olsson/PhotoAlto Agency RF Collections/Getty Images; p. 17 Nacivet/Photographer's Choice/Getty Images; p. 18 Pinkcandy/Shutterstock.com; p. 20 mimagephotography/Shutterstock.com; p. 22 © iStockphoto.com/BakiBG; p. 24 monkeybusinessimages/iStock/Thinkstock; p. 28 max-kegfire/iStock/Thinkstock; p. 30 Vitchanan Photography/Shutterstock.com; p. 31 JohnMartinBradley/iStock/Thinkstock; p. 33 skynesher/E+/Getty Images; p. 37 Peter Cade/The Image Bank/Getty Images; p. 42 Chinnapong/Shutterstock.com; p. 45 sturti/E+/Getty Images; p. 47 stockphoto mania/Shutterstock.com.

Design and Layout: Nicole Russo-Duca; Photo Research: Ellina Litmanovich